Learn to DRAW

Baby Animals

Jorge Santillan and Sarah Eason

WAYLAND

First published in 2015 by Wayland
Copyright © Wayland 2015

Wayland
338 Euston Road
London NW1 3BH

Wayland Australia
Level 17/207 Kent Street
Sydney, NSW 2000

Produced for Wayland by Calcium
Design by Paul Myerscough
Illustrations by Jorge Santillan

A catalogue record for this book is available from the British Library

Dewey classification: 743.6'91392-dc23

10 9 8 7 6 5 4 3 2 1

ISBN: 978 0 7502 9085 2
eBook ISBN: 978 0 7502 9087 6

Printed in China

Wayland is a division of Hachette Children's Books,
an Hachette UK company.
www.hachette.co.uk

Contents

Learn to Draw!

Baby animals are adorable! If you love animal babies, now you can learn how to draw them, too! From kittens and chicks to bunnies, puppies, lambs and frisky foals, discover the cutest, most lovable babies of the animal world!

4

You will need:

Just a few simple pieces of equipment are needed to create gorgeous drawings of baby animals:

Sketchpad or paper
Visit an art shop to buy good quality paper.

Pencils
You will need both fine-tipped and thick-tipped pencils.

Rubber
Don't worry if you make a mistake – use a rubber to remove any unwanted lines. You can even use it to add highlights.

Paintbrush, paints and pens
Buy a set of quality paints, brushes and colouring pens to add colour to your adorable drawings.

Playful Puppies

Dogs are loving and fun, and their babies are super sweet! Puppies love to have fun and will play with their owners for hours. Try a game of chase or fetch with a puppy, and it will be your friend forever!

Step 1

Draw your puppy in a crouching pose. Draw the shape of its body, then draw its legs, paws and tail. Next, draw the puppy's head and ears.

Step 2

Go over the rough lines from step 1 to draw the puppy's outline. Mark the eyes and the nose. Rub out the lines from step 1.

Step 3

Now draw the lines on the puppy's paws. Add more detail to the eyes, nose and muzzle. Give your puppy a collar.

Step 4

Pencil pupils in the puppy's eyes, add the whisker marks on its nose and the fine lines on its face and body.

Step 5

Now add shading to your puppy's body, legs, paws, ears, tail and face. Use deeper shading for the eyes and the nose.

Step 6

Colour your puppy with a rich brown shade. Add dark brown markings to the tail and back. Colour the puppy's eyes and ears a dark brown. Use a beige colour for the muzzle and paws, and a red for the collar. Give your puppy a golden name tag.

8

Step 7

Now you can put the finishing touches on your puppy. Colour its nose dark brown, then add white highlights to the puppy's eyes and brows. Add some highlights to its paws, ears, back and tail, too. Your cute puppy is complete!

Sleepy Puppies

Like all babies, puppies spend a lot of time sleeping. Baby dogs are born with their eyes shut, and they do not open them until they are around 11 days old! Between two and four weeks old, puppies start to wag their tails, growl and bark.

Cute Kittens

Tiny, fluffy and full of mischief, kittens are great fun to watch. These baby animals are furry balls of energy, and love to run around chasing after just about anything!

Step 1

Draw a square for the kitten's head, then draw its legs and body. Use triangles for the kitten's ears and draw a long, curving 'S' shape for its tail.

Step 2

Go over the lines you drew in step 1 to draw the curving outline of the kitten. Rub out any unwanted lines, then roughly mark the eyes, paws and nose.

Step 3

Now add more detail to the face. Draw the shape of the eyes, nose and mouth. Add the lines on the paws. Draw some fur around the face.

Step 4

Shade the pupils of the eyes. Draw the whiskers and add detail to the shape of the nose. Then draw an oval shape for the kitten's chest.

11

Step 5

Now add shading to the kitten's head, face, body, legs and tail. Shade more deeply around the neck and the kitten's belly.

Step 6

Your kitten is a ginger cat! Colour it with a rich orange shade, then add the darker orange markings on the head, legs, back and tail. Colour the ears dark orange and the chest, nose and mouth cream. Colour the kitten's eyes green.

Step 7

Add more shading to your kitten's body. Then put highlights on its eyes, chest, paws, tail and ears to finish your cute and furry friend.

Playful Kittens

Kittens spend lots of time play-fighting each other. It might look like they are just having fun, but this type of play helps baby cats learn how to hunt. Kittens love to play chase games, too. Try wiggling a piece of string across the floor and watch how a kitten darts after it!

Baby Bunnies

With their huge, round eyes, long, soft ears and twitching noses, it's easy to love baby bunnies! These babies love to be petted and stroked as long as they are handled very gently.

Step 1

Use a rounded shape for your bunny's head. Add two triangular shapes for the ears. Next, draw the body and legs. Then draw the bunny's tail.

Step 2

Go over the lines from step 1 to draw the outline. Rub out any unwanted lines. Mark the eye and nose. Add the lines on the head, body and ears.

Step 3

Now draw the shape of the bunny's eye, nose and mouth, then add the lines on the paws. Draw the tips of the bunny's ears.

Step 4

Shade the outline and pupil of the eye. Add whiskers and fur lines.

Step 5

Now add shading to your bunny's face, eye, ears, body and legs. Use darker shading for the eye.

Step 6

Colour some of your bunny dark grey, as shown. Use a light pinky-grey for the paler parts of the bunny. Colour the bunny's eye a rich, deep red.

Step 7

Now add highlights to your bunny's eye, ears, back and paws. Colour the inside of the ears pink. Add some touches of dark grey for extra shade.

Big Bunny Family

Bunnies have lots of babies. Rabbit mums can have many babies at once, and sometimes up to seven or eight babies at the same time! The group of baby bunnies is called a litter.

Lovable Lambs

Lambs are gentle babies that need lots of loving care from their mums. These babies must drink a lot of milk from their mothers after they are born, to help them grow big and strong. Lambs often twitch their fluffy tails as they drink their mum's milk!

Step 1

Draw a rectangular shape for the body. Then draw the legs, neck and head. Use triangular shapes for the ears and add the tail.

Step 2

Go over the lines you drew in step 1 to give your lamb a rounded outline. Mark the eyes and the nose. Rub out any unwanted lines from step 1.

18

Step 3

Now add the shape of the eyes, nose and mouth. Add detail to the ears and the hooves.

Step 4

Shade the eyes and add some markings to show the wool on the lamb's legs, body and tail.

Step 5

Add shading to your lamb's face, ears, legs and body. Use darker shading for the neck and the inner rear leg.

Step 6

Colour your lamb's body, legs, tail and ears with a beige shade. Leave the head white. Colour the hooves dark brown.

Step 7

Colour the inside of the ears pink. Then use a deep brown shade for the nose and the mouth. Add a little more shading and some highlights.

Springtime Babies

A female sheep is called a ewe. A ewe will often have more than one lamb at the same time. Some have two babies, called twins. Some even have three lambs, called triplets. Lambs are born in the spring.

Frisky Foals

A baby horse is called a foal. These beautiful baby animals have very long legs – a foal's legs are almost as long as those of a fully-grown horse! Foals love to run and jump on their strong, slender legs.

Step 1

Draw a rectangular shape for the foal's body. Then draw its neck, head, legs and long, curving tail.

Step 2

Pencil a curved outline for your foal. Then rub out the rough lines from step 1. Roughly draw the foal's eye, nose and ears.

Step 3

Add detail to the shape of the legs, hooves, ears and tail. Draw the shape of the eye and the foal's nostril. Draw the mane, too.

Step 4

Add detail to the foal's mane and add lines to its tail and face. Add the lines on the body.

Step 5

Add depth to your picture by shading the foal's body and face. Use some deeper shading for the inside rear leg, and the foal's eye and neck.

Step 6

Colour your foal with a light brown shade. Use a chestnut brown for the mane, tail and eyes. Colour the hooves with a dark brown shade.

Step 7

Now add highlights to the foal's eye, ears, head, body, legs, hooves and tail. Add some more shading. Your frisky foal is complete!

Growing Up

A male foal is called a colt and a female foal is called a filly. When a foal is one year old, it is called a yearling. Baby horses do not become fully grown until they are around four or five years old.

Cheeping Chicks

L ike all baby birds, chicks hatch from eggs laid by their mothers. The mother bird lays her eggs in a nest to keep them safe. The babies break out of their eggs by pecking at them with their beaks.

Step 1

Use circular shapes for the chick's head, body and the top of its legs. Next, draw the legs and feet. Then draw a triangle for the chick's beak.

Step 2

Go over the rough lines from step 1 to give your chick a rounded outline. Mark the eye and pencil the shape of the feet and wings.

Step 3

Now draw the beak and the shape of the eye. Add feather marks to the wings and add more detail to the chick's feet and claws.

Step 4

Shade the chick's eye and then add detail to its feathers, beak, legs and feet.

Step 5

Shade your chick's head and body. Add some shading to the legs and feet, too.

Step 6

Use a bright yellow colour for the chick's head, wings and body. Colour the legs, feet and beak orange.

Step 7

Add a touch of blue to your chick's eye, then put some highlights on the head, body, wings, legs and feet. Add a little more shading, and your cute, cheeping chick is complete!

Fluffy Feathers

Chicks are covered in lots of soft, fluffy feathers called down. The soft feathers keep the tiny baby bird warm. As the chick grows older, it loses its down and instead grows smoother feathers like its mum's.

Glossary

adorable cute and very easy to love

bark the sound a dog or puppy makes to show that it is excited or angry

beak the hard part on a bird's face. Birds use their beaks to peck at things

dart to move around very quickly

detail the fine lines on a drawing

eggs hard, round objects that are laid by female birds. Baby birds grow within eggs until they are ready to hatch

fetch to collect something, such as a ball or toy

growl a deep sound that dogs or puppies make when they are scared or angry

hatch to break out of an egg

highlights the light parts on a picture

hooves the hard parts on an animal's feet

hunt to track down an animal for food

laid pushed an egg out of the body

loving full of love and affection

mischief naughty or playful

nest a rounded shape made of twigs, moss and other natural objects. Birds make nests in which to lay their eggs

nostril an opening on an animal's head through which it breathes

pecking tapping at something with a beak. Birds peck with their beaks

petted stroked and cuddled

pose the position a person or creature is in

shading the dark markings on a picture

slender slim, not fat

spring the season that follows winter. Many baby animals are born in the spring

twitching moving part of the body very quickly

wag when an animal moves its tail from side to side to show it is happy

For More Information

Books

Beth Gunnell, *The Animal Colouring Book*, Buster Books, 2013

Kate Thompson, *Junior How to Draw Baby Animals*, Top That! Publishing, 2011

Robin Cuddy, *Learn to Draw Rainforest & Jungle Animals*, Walter Foster, 2013

Websites

Find out about all kinds of animals on National Geographic's website:
kids.nationalgeographic.com/kids/animals

Find out how to draw more animals at:
www.wedrawanimals.com

Have fun drawing even more animals at:
www.drawingnow.com/how-to-draw-animals.html

Index